**Martyn Payne**

C000155367

# The Christmas Story

**for families to share**

# Zechariah receives a promise

[11] Then an angel of the Lord appeared to him, standing at the right side of the altar of incense. [12] When Zechariah saw him, he was startled and was gripped with fear. [13] But the angel said to him: 'Do not be afraid, Zechariah; your prayer has been heard. Your wife Elizabeth will bear you a son, and you are to call him John. [14] He will be a joy and delight to you, and many will rejoice because of his birth, [15] for he will be great in the sight of the Lord. He is never to take wine or other fermented drink, and he will be filled with the Holy Spirit even before he is born. [16] He will bring back many of the people of Israel to the Lord their God. [17] And he will go on before the Lord, in the spirit and power of Elijah, to turn the hearts of the parents to their children and the disobedient to the wisdom of the righteous – to make ready a people prepared for the Lord.'

[18] Zechariah asked the angel, 'How can I be sure of this? I am an old man and my wife is well on in years.'

[19] The angel said to him, 'I am Gabriel. I stand in the presence of God, and I have been sent to speak to you and to tell you this good news. [20] And now you will be silent and not able to speak until the day this happens, because you did not believe my words, which will come true at their appointed time.'

LUKE 1:11–20

## Commentary

The dramatic story of how God stepped into the world in the person of Jesus Christ begins here in the innermost part of the temple, with an elderly priest called Zechariah. He shouldn't really have been surprised that an angel appeared to him. It was part of what he believed in and taught to others, but sometimes we can end up going through the routine of prayer and no longer expecting God to answer us, and certainly Zechariah didn't really seem to believe the tremendous message given to him. He and his wife were elderly and the idea of having a son seemed beyond belief, never mind the fact that this son would have a special job to do to bring people back to God and prepare the way for someone even more important. The angel's visit literally leaves him speechless until the child is born. Zechariah couldn't believe what he was being told, despite his own faith in God, but God still used him to father John – later known as 'the Baptist' – who would point the way to Jesus as God's way of speaking to the whole world.

## ⁇ Questions

▶ Do we just go through the motions of prayer sometimes, so that we aren't really ready to hear God speaking to us?

▶ What was Zechariah's son going to do, according to what the angel said?

▶ Why did Zechariah doubt the angel? Is it always wrong to have doubts?

▶ What do you think the angel looked like?

## Old Testament story link

An angel appears to a husband and wife and promises them the gift of a special son.

JUDGES 13:1–20

## Key verse

'He will make ready a people prepared for the Lord.'

LUKE 1:17

## Visual aid

It was behind the curtain in the Holy of Holies that Zechariah had the surprise of his life. If you can draw the curtains near to where you are reading this, take turns to hide a surprise item behind them. Can the others guess what is hidden each time?

 ## Activity idea

Zechariah wasn't able to speak after this encounter until John was born. He would have had to use sign language. Use the internet to learn some proper sign language for key words in the story, such as temple, curtain, worship, God, surprise, baby, family and parents. You could also play a game of charades, using a form of sign language to try to describe something that happened to you recently.

 ## Prayer idea

God interrupted Zechariah's prayer with a visit from an angel. How ready are we to let our prayer be broken into by God? Pray a familiar prayer together, such as the Lord's Prayer, pausing for a while after each line to give space for God to 'intervene'. Be ready to hear his voice in your head or perhaps 'see' a special picture with your imagination.

# An angel visits Mary

26 In the sixth month of Elizabeth's pregnancy, God sent the angel Gabriel to Nazareth, a town in Galilee, 27 to a virgin pledged to be married to a man named Joseph, a descendant of David. The virgin's name was Mary. 28 The angel went to her and said, 'Greetings, you who are highly favoured! The Lord is with you.'

29 Mary was greatly troubled at his words and wondered what kind of greeting this might be. 30 But the angel said to her, 'Do not be afraid, Mary, you have found favour with God. 31 You will conceive and give birth to a son, and you are to call him Jesus. 32 He will be great and will be called the Son of the Most High. The Lord God will give him the throne of his father David, 33 and he will reign over Jacob's descendants for ever; his kingdom will never end.'

34 'How will this be,' Mary asked the angel, 'since I am a virgin?'

35 The angel answered, 'The Holy Spirit will come on you, and the power of the Most High will overshadow you. So the holy one to be born will be called the Son of God. 36 Even Elizabeth your relative is going to have a child in her old age, and she who was said to be unable to conceive is in her sixth month. 37 For no word from God will ever fail.'

38 'I am the Lord's servant,' Mary answered. 'May your word to me be fulfilled.' Then the angel left her.

LUKE 1:26–38

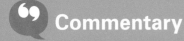 **Commentary**

What a surprising way for God to step into the world! Everyone longed for God to appear and put things right, but no one expected that it would involve a very ordinary young woman from an insignificant village in the poor north of a powerless country in the Middle East. God, who is called 'the most high' by the angel, chooses to send Jesus as a vulnerable, tiny baby to be brought up by a peasant family. No wonder Mary is overwhelmed. Even the angel seems awed by what God is about to do as he addresses Mary as 'truly blessed'.

Unlike Zechariah six months before, Mary doesn't doubt the angel; she is simply intrigued to know how she could have a son without a father. The answer is that this will be a miraculous birth in which God's Holy Spirit is at work. Mary's 'yes' is all that God needs, and it is on this that the rescue of the whole world depends. Heaven must have held its breath, waiting to hear what Mary would say to the angel; but this is how God always works, waiting for us to open our hearts to his plans for us and others. This is what can change everything.

8

## ?? Questions

- Do you think the angel was as surprised as Mary by God's choice of her?
- Why do you think the angel had to say to Mary, 'Don't be afraid'?
- What would this baby do, according to Gabriel's words?
- How was Mary reassured by Gabriel?
- Mary's 'yes' to God was so important. How might we say 'yes' to God today?

## Old Testament story link

Isaiah predicts the coming of a special baby to save the world.

ISAIAH 9:6–7

## Key verse

'No word from God will ever fail.'

LUKE 1:37

## Visual aid

Find a photo from the internet or cut out a picture from an aid magazine of a family living in a small one-room house in a very poor part of the world. Use it to remind you of the sort of place where Mary would have lived.

## Activity idea

Talk about some famous film and TV stories where superheroes or international organisations 'save the world', and wonder together about how many other ways God might have chosen to put the world right. What does this teach us about what God is like?

## Prayer idea

God's solution to the mess that human beings have made of our world wasn't a clever business plan, a super-strong army or a smart piece of technology, but a God-shaped baby called Jesus. Cut out some headlines from a newspaper about the ways in which our world is not the best it can be, and then place a picture of a baby (or perhaps a small baby doll) in the middle as you pray about those things. Let the baby be a focus to remind you of God's surprising way of responding to the problems around us.

# Mary visits Elizabeth

[39] At that time Mary got ready and hurried to a town in the hill country of Judea, [40] where she entered Zechariah's home and greeted Elizabeth. [41] When Elizabeth heard Mary's greeting, the baby leaped in her womb, and Elizabeth was filled with the Holy Spirit. [42] In a loud voice she exclaimed: 'Blessed are you among women, and blessed is the child you will bear! [43] But why am I so favoured, that the mother of my Lord should come to me? [44] As soon as the sound of your greeting reached my ears, the baby in my womb leaped for joy. [45] Blessed is she who has believed that the Lord would fulfil his promises to her!'

[46] And Mary said: 'My soul glorifies the Lord [47] and my spirit rejoices in God my Saviour, [48] for he has been mindful of the humble state of his servant. From now on all generations will call me blessed, [49] for the Mighty One has done great things for me – holy is his name. [50] His mercy extends to those who fear him, from generation to generation. [51] He has performed mighty deeds with his arm; he has scattered those who are proud in their inmost thoughts. [52] He has brought down rulers from their thrones but has lifted up the humble. [53] He has filled the hungry with good things but has sent the rich away empty. [54] He has helped his servant Israel, remembering to be merciful [55] to Abraham and his descendants for ever, just as he promised our ancestors.'

[56] Mary stayed with Elizabeth for about three months and then returned home.

LUKE 1:39–56

 # Commentary

Mary's three-month stay with her cousin Elizabeth would have been a good time to stay away from prying eyes in Nazareth, where people might have started asking awkward questions about her pregnancy. It gave her a chance to hear for herself Elizabeth's story; and perhaps it also gave time for Joseph, at home, to get his head around all that had happened.

The moment when the two cousins meet is a very special one indeed. Baby John 'leaps' for joy inside Elizabeth, and Elizabeth speaks powerful words of blessing over Mary, while Mary herself bursts into song, expressing her amazement and humility about the fact that God has chosen to honour the poor and powerless like her in his plans to save the world. The two women must have been such a support to each other during this time, not just sharing the ups and downs of pregnancy but also encouraging each other in prayer and worship because God was doing such great things in their lives and, through them, for the world.

# ?? Questions

▶ Although not yet born, it seems that the baby inside Elizabeth knew that Jesus was near. What does this tell us about the specialness of human life, even before birth?

▶ Elizabeth says several times that Mary is blessed. What does it mean to be blessed?

▶ What does Mary say about herself in her song, and what does she say about God?

▶ Elizabeth and Mary were not just relations but also special friends. How can you be a special friend to someone?

## Old Testament story link

This is what Hannah sang after she had received the gift of a child.

1 SAMUEL 2:1–10

## Key verse

'My soul glorifies the Lord.'
LUKE 1:46

# Visual aid

The meeting of Elizabeth and Mary is known as 'the visitation' and there are many famous pieces of artwork based on this story. Find one from the internet and use it as a focus for the reading today.

 # Activity idea

We know what Elizabeth and Mary said to each other when they first met, but I wonder what other conversations happened over the next months. How did they spend their time? Create an imaginary diary of their time together – where they went, what they bought, what they prayed about and who they met.

 # Prayer idea

Mary's song is also known as 'the Magnificat' (taken from the first word used in the Latin translation). It covers praise to God, thanks to God for his goodness, prayers to God for those who suffer because of powerful and oppressive governments, prayers for those who are facing hunger and prayers for those who need special help at the moment. Use this as a pattern for prayer.

# The birth of Jesus

¹ In those days Caesar Augustus issued a decree that a census should be taken of the entire Roman world. ² (This was the first census that took place while Quirinius was governor of Syria.) ³ And everyone went to their own town to register.

⁴ So Joseph also went up from the town of Nazareth in Galilee to Judea, to Bethlehem the town of David, because he belonged to the house and line of David. ⁵ He went there to register with Mary, who was pledged to be married to him and was expecting a child. ⁶ While they were there, the time came for the baby to be born, ⁷ and she gave birth to her firstborn, a son. She wrapped him in cloths and placed him in a manger, because there was no guest room available for them.

⁸ And there were shepherds living out in the fields near by, keeping watch over their flocks at night. ⁹ An angel of the Lord appeared to them, and the glory of the Lord shone around them, and they were terrified. ¹⁰ But the angel said to them, 'Do not be afraid. I bring you good news that will cause great joy for all the people. ¹¹ Today in the town of David a Saviour has been born to you; he is the Messiah, the Lord. ¹² This will be a sign to you: you will find a baby wrapped in cloths and lying in a manger.' ¹³ Suddenly a great company of the heavenly host appeared with the angel, praising God and saying, ¹⁴ 'Glory to God in the highest heaven, and on earth peace to those on whom his favour rests.' ¹⁵ When the angels had left them and gone into heaven, the shepherds said to one another, 'Let's go to Bethlehem and see this thing that has happened, which the Lord has told us about.'

LUKE 2:1–15

# Commentary

Luke gives us a detailed account of exactly when Jesus was born. The references to the emperor, the census and the governor are important because Luke wants us to know that this really happened and that it is not some made-up story. He is telling his readers that Jesus' coming into the world is something you can find in the history books and was something that has changed the world forever. This is what the angels mean when they surprise the poor shepherds on the hillside with their singing. Their song speaks of peace with God, which is now possible for anyone, whether they are carpenters, shepherds or emperors. But all this has to start with a baby lying on a bed of hay. The long journey south to Jerusalem must have been tough for Mary, but the fact that the baby was born in Bethlehem is an important clue to who Jesus really is. He will be a king, like David long ago, but also a different sort of king because his reign will not end with his death – but that part of the story is still to come!

# ?? Questions

▶ Can you imagine the conversations between Mary and Joseph when they received the news that they had to go to Bethlehem?

▶ Why do you think there was no room for Mary and Joseph when they arrived in Bethlehem?

▶ The job of being a shepherd wasn't particularly popular in those days. Why do you think God chose shepherds to be the first to hear the good news?

▶ What do you think the shepherds talked about after they had found the baby in Bethlehem?

▶ Which part of this Christmas story do you like best?

## Old Testament story link

This is Micah's prophecy of what would happen in Bethlehem one day.

MICAH 5:2–5

## Key verse

'Today in the town of David a Saviour has been born to you; he is the Messiah, the Lord.'

LUKE 2:11

## Visual aid

Find your nativity set, or a picture of the stable, among the Christmas decorations and wrapping paper that you have stored away. Use this as a focus for the story.

 ## Activity idea

Everyone is travelling in this story. Mary and Joseph and many others are on their way to somewhere else because of the emperor's command, and the shepherds are running off the hillside – even leaving their sheep behind, it seems. Pretend to be these different groups as they travel, and imagine their conversations with one another. What new insights and ideas about the story can you uncover? End by choosing your favourite Christmas carol and singing it together.

 ## Prayer idea

The angels' song expresses the joy in heaven that Jesus has been born. Think of all the good things that have happened to your family recently and, as you name them, say together, 'Glory to God in the highest'. Now think of all the places on earth where sad things are happening and, as you name them, pray together, 'May there be peace in…' and 'May people do what pleases God.'

# Simeon praises the Lord

22 When the time came for the purification rites
required by the Law of Moses, Joseph and Mary took him
to Jerusalem to present him to the Lord 23 (as it is written
in the Law of the Lord, 'Every firstborn male is to be consecrated to the
Lord'), 24 and to offer a sacrifice in keeping with what is said in the Law of the Lord:
'a pair of doves or two young pigeons'.

25 Now there was a man in Jerusalem called Simeon, who was righteous and
devout. He was waiting for the consolation of Israel, and the Holy Spirit was
on him. 26 It had been revealed to him by the Holy Spirit that he would not die
before he had seen the Lord's Messiah. 27 Moved by the Spirit, he went into the
temple courts. When the parents brought in the child Jesus to do for him what
the custom of the Law required, 28 Simeon took him in his arms and praised God,
saying:

29 'Sovereign Lord, as you have promised, you may now dismiss your servant in
peace. 30 For my eyes have seen your salvation, 31 which you have prepared in the
sight of all nations: 32 a light for revelation to the Gentiles, and the glory of your
people Israel.'

33 The child's father and mother marvelled at what was said about him. 34 Then
Simeon blessed them and said to Mary, his mother: 'This child is destined to
cause the falling and rising of many in Israel, and to be a sign that will be spoken
against, 35 so that the thoughts of many hearts will be revealed. And a sword will
pierce your own soul too.'

LUKE 2:22-35

# Commentary

All life is a gift from God, and every child is a sign of God's generous love to the world. To help people remember this, the Jewish laws said that the firstborn child in a family 'belonged to God' and that there needed to be a special ceremony to celebrate the birth. Jesus was Mary's firstborn son and, because Bethlehem wasn't far from the temple in Jerusalem, they went there for the service; however, it didn't turn out quite as they expected. An elderly man called Simeon turned up and began singing praises to God about how special Jesus would be. Simeon was a man of prayer and, like many in Israel, was waiting for God to come and rescue his country, just as the promises in the Old Testament said would happen one day. Simeon had the faith to recognise that this rescue had arrived in the shape of a baby and he rejoiced to have seen him. He sang about what Jesus would do, but also spoke some sad words to Mary, because the way Jesus would one day rescue the world would break her heart. Can you work out why?

# ?? Questions

▶ This story takes place about six weeks after Christmas, at the beginning of February on our calendar. What new things about Jesus do we learn from what Simeon said?

▶ What sort of man was Simeon?

▶ Mary and Joseph always knew that Jesus was special and that he was from God, so why were they surprised by what Simeon told them?

▶ Mary and Joseph brought doves to say 'thank you' to God for the gift of a new baby. What could you give to God to say 'thank you' for something?

## Old Testament story link

This is Isaiah's song about the child who will come as the true king to rescue everyone one day.

ISAIAH 11:1–9

## Key verse

'Your salvation… [is] a light for revelation to the Gentiles.'

LUKE 2:30, 32

# Visual aid

Use a walking stick as a way to introduce old man Simeon, who had been waiting patiently all his life to meet Jesus.

 # Activity idea

Simeon sang a song of praise to God as he held the baby Jesus – his very own, belated Christmas carol. He talks about Jesus being a light for the whole world. Cut out a picture of the earth and then pierce it all over with tiny pinpricks. Hold it carefully in front of a candle or a small light in a dark corner of the room and see how the whole world is lit up.

 # Prayer idea

Take it in turns to compose a short prayer of thanks for every person in your family. Thank God for each person's personality, gifts, funny ways, support and love. Make sure that everyone has a chance to offer a thank-you prayer in this way, for someone else rather than themselves.

# Herod and the wise men

[1] After Jesus was born in Bethlehem in Judea, during the time of King Herod, Magi from the east came to Jerusalem [2] and asked, 'Where is the one who has been born king of the Jews? We saw his star when it rose and have come to worship him.' [3] When King Herod heard this he was disturbed, and all Jerusalem with him. [4] When he had called together all the people's chief priests and teachers of the law, he asked them where the Messiah was to be born. [5] 'In Bethlehem in Judea,' they replied, 'for this is what the prophet has written: [6] "But you, Bethlehem, in the land of Judah, are by no means least among the rulers of Judah; for out of you will come a ruler who will shepherd my people Israel."'

[7] Then Herod called the Magi secretly and found out from them the exact time the star had appeared. [8] He sent them to Bethlehem and said, 'Go and search carefully for the child. As soon as you find him, report to me, so that I too may go and worship him.'

[9] After they had heard the king, they went on their way, and the star they had seen when it rose went ahead of them until it stopped over the place where the child was. [10] When they saw the star, they were overjoyed. [11] On coming to the house, they saw the child with his mother Mary, and they bowed down and worshipped him. Then they opened their treasures and presented him with gifts of gold, frankincense and myrrh. [12] And having been warned in a dream not to go back to Herod, they returned to their country by another route.

MATTHEW 2:1–12

# Commentary

This story could have taken place any time up to two years after the birth of Jesus. Mary and Joseph were living in a house in Bethlehem and their eastern visitors had clearly been following the star for quite some time. They were astrologers – people who studied and found special meanings in the patterns and the brightness of the stars – and the new star that guided them was, in their understanding, the signpost to a new king. Understandably, they looked for this royal baby in a palace, but Jesus was going to be a different sort of king. Bethlehem was the birthplace of King David long ago and it was there that Herod's advisers sent the wise men.

Their arrival is a reminder that this child was going to be a gift for the whole world, and the special presents have become symbolic of the work Jesus came to do as the bringer of the kingdom of God (gold), the way to the true worship of God (frankincense) and the means by which people would find God's healing from all that was wrong inside (myrrh). These wise men from the east were among the first people to seek Jesus and, as an old saying goes, wise people still seek him.

# ⁇ Questions

▶ Why do you think Herod was so worried when he heard what the wise men were asking about?

▶ What clues in the story can you find that Herod didn't actually want to go and worship the child?

▶ Frankincense was used in worship, and the sweet-smelling perfume of myrrh helped to overcome the smell of disease and death. Why do you think the wise men gave these particular gifts?

▶ Do you think Mary and Joseph used these gifts, or did they keep them safe as a reminder of the visit?

# Old Testament story link

Long ago, Isaiah wrote about visitors from far away who would come with gold and spices to worship God.

ISAIAH 60:4–6

## Key verse

'They bowed down and worshipped him.'

MATTHEW 2:11

# Visual aid

Light a fragrant candle and enjoy its aroma. This is like the frankincense that was given. Perhaps you can find a gold ring and some perfume to represent the other two gifts, as well.

 # Activity idea

From a book or the internet, find a picture of the night sky in your part of the world. Pick out the brightest stars and the faintest ones; can you see any patterns in the stars? Identify the Pole Star and some other well-known constellations. Imagine the excitement there would be if a brand-new star appeared suddenly. If possible, go out and look at the night sky.

Planets look like stars in the sky but they don't twinkle. Can you find any?

 # Prayer idea

Use the three gifts as a prompt for you to worship Jesus together. Gold is for honouring him as king in our lives; frankincense is for recognising Jesus as the one who shows us God; myrrh is for healing all our ills and pains. Combine these ideas in a simple prayer: 'King Jesus, bring us closer to God each day. Heal us and forgive us for all the things we have done that have hurt you and others.'

# The escape to Egypt

¹³ When they had gone, an angel of the Lord appeared to Joseph in a dream. 'Get up,' he said, 'take the child and his mother and escape to Egypt. Stay there until I tell you, for Herod is going to search for the child to kill him.'

¹⁴ So he got up, took the child and his mother during the night and left for Egypt, ¹⁵ where he stayed until the death of Herod. And so was fulfilled what the Lord had said through the prophet: 'Out of Egypt I called my son.'

¹⁶ When Herod realised that he had been outwitted by the Magi, he was furious, and he gave orders to kill all the boys in Bethlehem and its vicinity who were two years old and under, in accordance with the time he had learned from the Magi. ¹⁷ Then what was said through the prophet Jeremiah was fulfilled: ¹⁸ 'A voice is heard in Ramah, weeping and great mourning, Rachel weeping for her children and refusing to be comforted, because they are no more.'

¹⁹ After Herod died, an angel of the Lord appeared in a dream to Joseph in Egypt ²⁰ and said, 'Get up, take the child and his mother and go to the land of Israel, for those who were trying to take the child's life are dead.'

²¹ So he got up, took the child and his mother and went to the land of Israel. ²² But when he heard that Archelaus was reigning in Judea in place of his father Herod, he was afraid to go there. Having been warned in a dream, he withdrew to the district of Galilee, ²³ and he went and lived in a town called Nazareth. So was fulfilled what was said through the prophets, that he would be called a Nazarene.

MATTHEW 2:13–23

 **Commentary**

Jesus didn't have the best of starts in life. There was no room in the inn; his first cot was an animal feeding box; his parents were far from friends and the wider family; and now Jesus becomes a refugee in a foreign country. Even during his first years on earth, Jesus experienced the risks and discomforts that many families experience every single day. God in Jesus was not protected from the dangers of this world, and therefore he can understand the bad times that we all go through.

Herod's power-mad jealousy leads him to order one of the most terrible crimes in history, as innocent children are killed and their parents left in tears. Jesus should have been with them, and indeed he will be killed one day, but his time has not yet come. The story is written in such a way as to remind us again and again that God has a plan, promised long ago; all this is slowly but surely being worked out as the holy family are kept safe and, after several years, are guided back to Nazareth where their story began.

## ?? Questions

▶ God uses dreams several times in the story as a way to speak to Joseph. Long ago, another Joseph had dreams that came true. Can you recall this story and what happened?

▶ Can you remember any special dreams you have had?

▶ How does Matthew, the writer, make it clear in this story that God is in control?

▶ Why did God choose to speak in dreams to Joseph, and not to Mary?

## Old Testament story link

Moses was another child who faced death at the beginning of his life, but escaped miraculously and went on to become a great leader.

EXODUS 2:1–9

## Key verse

'He went and lived in a town called Nazareth. So was fulfilled what was said through the prophets.'

MATTHEW 2:23

#  Visual aid

Find a map of the Middle East and trace Mary and Joseph's escape route from Bethlehem to Egypt and then back to Nazareth.

#  Activity idea

Imagine that Joseph kept a diary of his escape with the family from Bethlehem to Egypt and then home again. Make up some possible diary entries for the journey. Where did they stay? Who did they meet? How did they feel? Did they use the wise men's gifts or not? What problems did they face? What was their scariest moment? What was their most difficult decision? What were their greatest worries? How did they keep trusting God?

#  Prayer idea

Many people today are forced to leave their homeland because of war or natural disaster, to become refugees in another country. Find out about one such refugee group and pray for them. Ask that they might know God's help in the middle of their troubles. Jesus has experienced what it is like to be a refugee and is ready to support them.

# The Lord's Prayer

Jesus said, 'Pray then in this way:

> Our Father in heaven,
>> hallowed be your name.
>> Your kingdom come.
>> Your will be done,
>>> on earth as it is in heaven.
>> Give us this day our daily bread.
>> And forgive us our debts,
>>> as we also have forgiven our debtors.
>> And do not bring us to the time of trial,
>>> but rescue us from the evil one.'

MATTHEW 6:9–13 (NRSV)

15 The Chambers, Vineyard
Abingdon OX14 3FE
**brf.org.uk**

Bible Reading Fellowship is a charity (233280)
and company limited by guarantee (301324),
registered in England and Wales

ISBN 978 1 80039 120 8
First published 2021
Reprinted 2022
10 9 8 7 6 5 4 3 2 1
All rights reserved

### Acknowledgements
Unless otherwise stated, scripture quotations taken from The Holy Bible, New
International Version Anglicised Copyright © 1979, 1984, 2011 Biblica. Used by
permission of Hodder & Stoughton Ltd, an Hachette UK company. All rights reserved.
'NIV' is a registered trademark of Biblica UK trademark number 1448790.

Scripture quotation marked NRSV is taken from The New Revised Standard Version
of the Bible, Anglicised edition, copyright © 1989, 1995 by the Division of Christian
Education of the National Council of the Churches of Christ in the United States of
America. Used by permission. All rights reserved.

Every effort has been made to trace and contact copyright owners for material used
in this resource. We apologise for any inadvertent omissions or errors, and would ask
those concerned to contact us so that full acknowledgement can be made in the future.

A catalogue record for this book is available from the British Library

Printed and bound in the UK by Zenith Media NP4 0DQ